O9-BTI-842

BOSTON COMMON PRESS
Brookline, Massachusetts

1999

Copyright © 1999 by The Editors of *Cook's Illustrated*

All rights reserved. No part of this book may be reproduced or transmitted in any manner whatsoever without written permission from the publisher, except in the case of brief quotations embodied in critical articles or reviews.

Boston Common Press
17 Station Street
Brookline, Massachusetts 02445

ISBN 0-936184-29-9
Library of Congress Cataloging-in-Publication Data
The Editors of *Cook's Illustrated*

How to make stew: An illustrated step-by-step guide to beef, lamb, pork, chicken, seafood, and vegetable stews./The Editors of *Cook's Illustrated*
1st ed.

Includes 24 recipes and 19 illustrations
ISBN 0-936184-29-9 (hardback): $14.95
I. Cooking. I. Title
1999

Manufactured in the United States of America

Distributed by Boston Common Press, 17 Station Street, Brookline, MA 02445.

Cover and text design: Amy Klee
Recipe development: Dawn Yanagihara
Series editor: Jack Bishop

HOW
TO MAKE
STEW

An illustrated step-by-step guide to
beef, lamb, pork, chicken, seafood,
and vegetable stews.

THE COOK'S ILLUSTRATED LIBRARY

Illustrations by John Burgoyne

CONTENTS

introduction

S tews are eminently practical yet have an aspect of the divine as well, a pleasing marriage of parsimony and inspiration. The simple farmhouse can be home to a rustic beef stew made with whatever is on hand, while a fancy New York restaurant can hold its head high serving a daube or a fancy fish stew such as zarzuela.

Yet what seems to be quite a simple dish is actually anything but elementary. Which cuts of meat or types of fish are best for a stew? What is the secret of producing tender stew meat? Should a stew be barely simmered, or can it stand more vigorous heat? Does the surrounding liquid actually help the meat to retain moisture, or is it simply the makings of a sauce? Which is the best place to cook a stew, the stovetop or the oven? How do the properties of different foods such as chicken or fish affect the preparation of a stew? These are all questions we had to answer before developing recipes, and although this is a diminutive book in size and pages, you will find it complete with answers to those questions and many more.

Once we decided on the basic elements of a stew, we went on to create a wide array of recipes, from pork vindaloo to beef goulash to chicken stews to a Sicilian fish stew. By holding onto the thread of common techniques, we have linked recipes that are not often thought to stand on common ground. Most of us would not think of bouillabaisse and Irish stew as cousins.

Cook's Illustrated has published a number of books in this series, including *How to Make a Pie, How to Make an American Layer Cake, How to Stir-Fry, How to Make Ice Cream, How to Make Pizza, How to Make Holiday Desserts, How to Make Pasta Sauces, How to Make Salad, How to Grill, How to Make Simple Fruit Desserts, How to Make Cookie Jar Favorites,* and *How to Cook Holiday Roasts and Birds,* and many other titles in this series will soon be available. To order other books, call us at (800) 611-0759. We are also the editors and publishers of *Cook's Illustrated,* a bimonthly publication about American home cooking. For a free trial copy of *Cook's,* call (800) 526-8442.

Christopher P. Kimball
Publisher and Editor
Cook's Illustrated

chapter one

ℨ

STEW BASICS

OOD STEW IS HARD TO BEAT. WHEN SUCCESS-ful, stew is one of those dishes that is more than the sum of its parts. Slow, long cooking transforms proteins, vegetables, and liquids into a hearty, rugged dish that is satisfying and intensely flavored.

So what exactly is stew and how does it differ from soup or a braise? There is some disagreement in the food world, but for our purposes a stew is small chunks of meat, chicken, seafood, and/or vegetables cooked in liquid, which is usually thickened and served as a sauce. A stew is a one-dish meal that can be eaten with a fork and without a knife.

8

Soup may contain the same ingredients (small bits of protein and vegetables in a liquid base), but it contains much more liquid than a stew and the liquid is generally not thickened. Soup is eaten with a spoon.

At the opposite end of the spectrum is a braise, which usually contains less liquid than a stew and the protein and vegetables are cut into much larger pieces or even left whole, as in a pot roast. The meat in a braise often contains bones (stews are usually boneless) and the vegetables are more for flavoring the meat and juices than for eating. Finally, a braise is eaten with a fork but usually requires a knife as well.

Stews and braises do have a number of elements in common—the aromatic vegetables (as well as the meat and chicken) are usually browned and the cooking temperature must be low. Browning is important because it develops flavor. The sugars in the vegetables (and the meat and chicken) caramelize in a process known as the Maillard reaction. Deglazing the pan with wine or stock loosens flavorful browned bits from the bottom of the pan, which in turn dissolve and flavor the stew liquid.

Contrary to popular belief, browning does not seal in juices in stew meat. As the internal temperature of the meat rises, more and more juices are expelled. By the time the meat is fork-tender, it has shed most of its juices. As odd it sounds, this is the beauty of a stew or braise because the surrounding liquid, which will be served as a sauce, is enriched by these juices.

Stew meat remains edible because slow-cooking turns the collagen and connective tissue found in tough cuts of meat, such as the beef shoulder or chicken thighs, into gelatin. This gelatin makes meat tender; it also helps thicken the stew liquid. The same thing happens when these tough cuts are barbecued or slow-roasted. Prolonged low-temperature cooking allows the connective tissue to break down and makes the meat tender.

The main difference between slow-roasting and stewing is that in stewing the exterior of the meat is less likely to dry out and overcook in the liquid. That's because the temperature of the stewing or braising liquid cannot exceed 212 degrees, or the boiling point. This ceiling limits the rate at which the meat can cook.

In our testing, we found that the temperature of the stewing liquid is crucial when certain ingredients are stewed. We found it is essential to keep the temperature of the liquid below 212 degrees when stewing meat or chicken. If either is boiled, it stays tough and the outside becomes especially dry. Keeping the liquid at a simmer (rather than a boil) allows the internal temperature of the meat to rise slowly. By the time it is actually fork-tender, much of the collagen will have turned to gelatin.

We have found that putting a covered Dutch oven in a 250-degree oven ensures that the temperature of the stewing liquid will remain below the boiling point, at about 200 degrees. (Ovens are not totally effective at transferring heat; a temperature of 250 degrees recognizes that some heat will be lost as it penetrates through the pot and into the stew.)

The temperature of the liquid is crucial when making fish stew, but for a different reason. Since fish is so delicate and cooks so quickly, it is added to stews just before serving. (The deep seafood flavor comes from the stock, not the fish itself used in the stew.) We find it best to cook the fish for a few minutes in the liquid, then turn off the burner and cover the pot. The fish finishes cooking in the residual heat and is less likely to become dry or fall apart.

When making vegetable stews, temperature is not nearly as important since the main goal is to soften the vegetables to an appealing texture. You don't want to boil a vegetable stew so furiously that the vegetables fall apart. A brisk simmer is fine for all-vegetable stews.

INGREDIENTS FOR MAKING STEW

The meat, chicken, seafood, and/or vegetables are the most important ingredients in any stew. Buying the right cuts and preparing them for stewing are discussed in the appropriate chapters.

In addition to the "main ingredients," there are a number of supporting ingredients that appear again and again in recipes throughout this book. These ingredients are the basis for the sauce that surrounds the main stew ingredients. In particular, we find the choice of canned broth, canned tomatoes, and wine to be important when making a stew.

፨ BROTH Homemade stock makes delicious stews. However, with the exception of fish stews, we find that canned products will work quite well and they greatly simplify the process. (Fish stew can be made with doctored-up bottled clam juice, with some sacrifice in flavor.) There is no reason not to use homemade stock if you have some on hand, but beef, chicken, lamb, pork, and vegetable stews will taste just fine if made with a carefully selected canned broth.

You might think that meat stews, especially those with beef, would taste better when made with canned beef broth. However, canned beef broths simply do not deliver full-bodied, beefy flavor. We tested 11 commercial beef broths and bouillon cubes. Some had a subtle suggestion of beef, but most begged the question, "Where's the beef?"

Current government regulations require that beef broth need only contain 1 part protein to 135 parts moisture. That translates to less than one ounce of meat to flavor a gallon of water. Most manufacturers use salt, monosodium glutamate (MSG), and yeast-based hydrolyzed soy protein to give this watery concoction some flavor and mouthfeel. Does any canned beef broth or powdered beef bouillon cube taste like the real thing? Our panel shouted a resounding no.

By comparison, canned chicken broths are far superior. While they rarely taste like homemade stock, several of the 11 brands that we tested had some decent chicken flavor. In stews, even those made with beef, we found that canned chicken broth is superior to canned beef broth. So which canned broths do we recommend? In our tasting, reduced-sodium and low-sodium broths made by Campbell's and Swanson (both brands are owned by the same company) topped the list.

TOMATOES Chopped tomatoes are used in many stews in place of wine to add an acidic element, color, and flavor. We find that canned tomatoes are easier to work with than fresh (which would have to be peeled before chopping) and their flavor is usually better. If you have some very good ripe tomatoes on hand and don't mind peeling them, go ahead and use them. However, canned tomatoes are fine for every recipe in this book.

Our favorite canned tomato product is Muir Glen Diced Tomatoes. These tomatoes are convenient to use, since they have already been chopped, and the flavor is especially fresh and bright with a good balance of sweet and acid flavors. Whole canned tomatoes can be used as well. Simply remove the tomatoes from their liquid, chop, and measure. When buying canned whole tomatoes, we recommend choosing brands packed in tomato juice, not tomato puree. The puree gives the tomato a cooked flavor that we don't generally like. In our testing of leading brands, Muir Glen and Progresso whole tomatoes came out on top.

:: WINE We found in our testing that the quality of the wine used in a stew matters. "Cooking wine"—the dreadful, usually oxidized stuff sold in supermarkets—does not cut it when it comes to a stew that relies on wine for much of its flavor. However, there is no reason to overcompensate. Pouring a $30 bottle of good burgundy or Cabernet Sauvignon into the pot is not advisable either. We found that as long as the wine tastes good enough to drink, it will make delicious stew. Therefore, we recommend inexpensive, young wines in the $7 to $9 range when making stew. In general, fruity reds such as Chianti, zinfandel, young cabernets from California, and many of the hearty wines from southern France are best in stew. As for white wines, avoid those which are very dry or heavily oaked. A crisp, fruity Sauvignon Blanc, Pinot Blanc, or a young Chardonnay is ideal.

14

EQUIPMENT FOR MAKING STEW

Other than some spoons and ladles, stew making doesn't require much in the way of equipment. Of course, you need a cutting board and some knives to chop ingredients, but otherwise the focus is on the pot.

We found that a Dutch oven (also called a lidded casserole) is almost essential for making a stew. You can try to use a large pasta pot or soup kettle, but these pots are probably too narrow and tall. Also, many are quite light, thin, and cheap—designed to heat up water quickly but not meant for browning. Since most stew recipes begin by browning to develop flavor, it's imperative to use a pot with a heavy bottom.

A Dutch oven (*see* figure 1, page 17) is nothing more than a wide, deep pot with a cover. It was originally manufactured with "ears" on the side (small, round tabs used to pick up the pot) and a top that had a lip around the edge. The latter design element was important because a Dutch oven was heated through coals placed both underneath and on top of the pot. The lip kept the coals on the lid from falling off. One could bake biscuits, cobblers, beans, and stews in this pot. It was, in the full sense of the word, an oven. This oven was a key feature of chuck wagons and essential in many American homes where all cooking occurred in the fireplace. As for the word "Dutch," it seems that the best cast iron came from Holland and the pots were therefore referred to as Dutch ovens.

Now that everyone in America has an oven, the Dutch oven is no longer used to bake biscuits or cobblers. However, it is essential for dishes that start on top of the stove and finish in the oven, like stew. In order to make some recommendations about buying a modern Dutch oven, we tested 12 models made by leading cookware companies.

In our testing, we found that a Dutch oven should have a capacity of at least six quarts to be useful. (Eight quarts is even better.) As we cooked in the pots, we came to prefer wider and shallower Dutch ovens because they make it easier to check the progress of the cooking. They also offer more bottom surface to accommodate larger batches of meat for browning. This reduces the number of batches required to brown a given quantity of meat, and with it, the chances of burning the flavorful pan drippings. Ideally, a Dutch oven should have a diameter twice as wide as its height.

We also preferred pots with a light-colored interior finish, such as stainless steel or enameled cast iron. It is easier to judge the caramelization of the drippings at a glance in these pots. Dark finishes can mask the color of the drippings, which may burn before you realize it. Our favorite pot is the eight-quart All-Clad Stainless Stockpot (despite the name, this pot is a Dutch oven). The seven-quart Le

Creuset Round French Oven, which is made of enameled cast-iron, also tested well. These pots are quite expensive, costing at least $150, even when on sale. The seven-quart Lodge Dutch Oven is made from cast-iron. It is extremely heavy (making it a bit hard to maneuver) and it must be seasoned regularly. The dark interior finish is also not ideal. But is browns ingredients quite well and costs just $45.

Figure 1.

The ideal Dutch oven is twice as wide as it is high. It also should have handles on both sides (to make it easy to lift the pot in and out of the oven) as well as a lid with a handle. Since this pot often goes into the oven, make sure that the handles are ovenproof.

chapter two

෩

MEAT STEWS

EAT STEWS, MADE WITH BEEF, LAMB, OR pork, should be rich and satisfying. Our goal in developing a master recipe for meat stew was to keep the cooking process simple without compromising the stew's deep, complex flavor.

At the outset, we made several decisions. We tried several recipes with homemade meat stock. They were delicious but require much more effort than stews made with canned broth or other liquids. At the other extreme, we rejected recipes that call for dumping meat, vegetables, and liquid into a pot to simmer for a couple of hours. Browning the meat and some of the vegetables, especially onions, adds flavor, and this step is too important to skip.

We focused on the following issues: What cut or cuts of meat respond best to stewing? Is it the same cut from different animals? How much and what kind of liquid should you use? When and with what do you thicken the stew? And where should the stew be cooked, in the oven or on top of the stove, or does it matter?

We decided to start our tests with beef and then see if our findings held true for lamb and pork. We sampled 12 different cuts of beef (*see* figure 2, page 25). We browned each, marked them for identification, and stewed them in the same pot. Chuck proved to be the most flavorful, tender, and juicy. Most other cuts were either too stringy, too chewy, too dry, or just plain bland. The exception was rib eye steak, which made good stew meat but is too expensive a cut to use for this purpose.

Our advice is to buy a steak or roast from the chuck and cube it yourself instead of buying precut stewing beef. The reason is simple: Prepackaged stewing beef is often made up of irregularly shaped end pieces from different muscles that cannot be sold retail as steaks or roasts because of their uneven appearance. Because of the differences in origin, precut stewing cubes in the same package may have inconsistent cooking, flavor, and tenderness qualities. If you cut your own cubes from a piece of chuck, you are assured that all the cubes will cook in the same way and have the flavor and richness of chuck.

The names given to different cuts of chuck vary, but the most commonly used names for retail chuck cuts include boneless chuck-eye roasts, cross-rib roasts, blade steaks and roasts, shoulder steaks and roasts, and arm steaks and roasts. We particularly liked chuck-eye roast in our testing, but all chuck cuts were delicious when cubed and stewed.

So why does chuck make the best stew? The intramuscular fat and connective tissue in chuck is well suited to long, slow, moist cooking. When cooked in liquid, the connective tissue melts down into gelatin, making the meat juicy and tender. The fat helps, too, in two important ways. Fat carries the chemical compounds that our taste buds receive as beef flavor, and it also melts when cooked, lubricating the meat fibers as it slips between the cells, increasing tenderness.

With our cut of beef settled, we started to explore how and when to thicken the stew. We tried several thickening methods and found most acceptable, with the exception of quick-cooking tapioca, which produced a slimy and gelatinous stew. Dredging meat cubes in flour is another roundabout way of thickening stew. The floured beef is browned, then stewed. During the stewing process, some of the flour from the beef dissolves into the liquid, causing it to thicken. Although the stew we cooked this way thickened up nicely, the beef cubes had a "smothered steak" look: The flour coating had browned, not the meat. This coating often fell off during cooking to expose pale and therefore less flavorful meat.

We also tried two thickening methods at the end of cooking—a beurre manié (softened butter mixed with flour) and cornstarch mixed with water. Either method is acceptable, but the beurre manié lightened the stew's color, making it look more like pale gravy than rich stew juices. Also, the extra fat did not improve the stew's flavor enough to justify it. For those who prefer thickening at the end of cooking, we found cornstarch dissolved in water did the job without compromising the stew's dark, rich color.

Pureeing the cooking vegetables is another thickening method. Once the stew is fully cooked, the meat is pulled from the pot and the juices and vegetables are pureed to create a thick sauce. We felt this thickening method made the vegetable flavor too prominent.

Ultimately, we opted for thickening the stew with flour at the beginning—stirring it into the sautéing onions and garlic, right before adding the liquid. Stew thickened this way did not taste any better, but it was easier to make. There's no last-minute work; once the liquid starts to simmer, the cook is free to do something else.

2 1

We next focused on stewing liquids. We tried water, wine, low-sodium canned beef broth, low-sodium chicken broth, as well as combinations of these liquids. Stews made with water were bland and greasy. Stews made with all wine were too strong. All stock was good, but we missed the acidity and flavor provided by the wine. In the end, we preferred a combination of chicken stock and red wine. (In general, we think canned chicken stock tastes better than canned beef stock; *see* page 12 for more information.)

We tested various amounts of liquid and found that we preferred stews with a minimum of liquid, as this preserves a strong meat flavor. With too little liquid, however, the stew may not cook evenly and there may not be enough stew "sauce" to spoon over starchy accompaniments. A cup of liquid per pound of meat gave us sufficient sauce to moisten a mound of mashed potatoes or polenta without drowning them.

We tested various kinds of wine and found that fairly inexpensive fruity, full-bodied young wines, such as Chianti, zinfandel, or cabernets were best. (*See* page 14 for more information on wine.)

In order to determine when to add the vegetables, we made three different stews, adding carrots, potatoes, and onions to one stew at the beginning of cooking and to another stew halfway through the cooking process. For our final stew, we cooked the onions with the meat but added steamed carrots and potatoes when the stew was fully cooked.

The stew with vegetables added at the beginning was thin and watery. The vegetables had fallen apart and given up their flavor and liquid to the stew. The beef stew with the cooked vegetables added at the last minute was delicious and the vegetables were the freshest and most intensely flavored. However, it is more work to steam the vegetables separately. Also, vegetables cooked separately from the stew don't really meld all that well with the other flavors and ingredients. We prefer to add the vegetables partway through the cooking process. They don't fall apart this way and they still have enough time to meld with the other stew ingredients. There is one exception to this rule. Peas should be added just before serving the stew to preserve their fresh color and texture.

Our recipe was now complete and we only had to fiddle with the cooking times and temperatures. We focused on low-temperature cooking methods, since we already knew that high heat toughens and dries out meat. We cooked stews on the stovetop over low heat (with and without a flame-taming device) and in a 250-degree oven. (You want to maintain a simmer in the pot, with temperatures staying below the boiling point, 212 degrees, so that the meat does not become tough and dry.)

The flame-tamer device worked too well and the stew

juices tasted raw and boozy. Putting the pot right on the burner worked better, but we had the most consistent results in the oven. We found ourselves constantly adjusting the burner to maintain a gentle simmer and this method is prone to error. Cooking in a 250-degree oven ensures a constant level of heat.

Regardless of whether you cook the stew on the stovetop or in the oven, the meat passes from the tough to tender stage fairly quickly. Often at the 2½-hour mark the meat would still be chewy. Fifteen minutes later it would be tender. Let the stew go another 15 minutes and the meat starts to dry out.

With a recipe using beef chuck developed, we wondered if the same technique and ingredients would work with other meats. We tested various cuts of pork and lamb and found that shoulder cuts respond best to stewing. Like chuck, these cuts have enough fat to keep the meat tender and juicy during the long cooking process.

Pork shoulder is often called Boston butt or Boston shoulder in markets. We generally bought a boneless Boston butt or pork shoulder roast (*see* figure 3, page 26) and cut it into cubes ourselves. A lamb shoulder roast can be hard to find. We often bought inexpensive bone-in lamb shoulder chops (*see* figure 4, page 27) and cut the meat off the bone and into chunks.

For the most part, the beef recipe worked fine with these cuts of pork and lamb. However, lamb tends to cook a bit more quickly. Beef and pork require a total cooking time of 2½ to 3 hours. Lamb needs just 2 to 2½ hours to soften up. All times will vary depending on the addition of slow-cooking vegetables, such as potatoes and carrots, as the meat cooks.

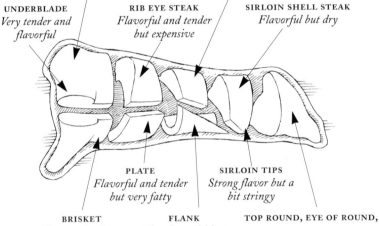

TOP BLADE
Most flavorful and tender

TENDERLOIN
Dried out in long cooking process

UNDERBLADE
Very tender and flavorful

RIB EYE STEAK
Flavorful and tender but expensive

SIRLOIN SHELL STEAK
Flavorful but dry

PLATE
Flavorful and tender but very fatty

SIRLOIN TIPS
Strong flavor but a bit stringy

BRISKET
Very tough, almost inedible

FLANK
Very flavorful but stringy

TOP ROUND, EYE OF ROUND, AND BOTTOM ROUND
Very dry, chewy, and bland

Figure 2.
We stewed 12 different cuts of beef from every part of the cow. Chuck, which consists of the underblade and top blade, was the most flavorful and cooked up quite tender.

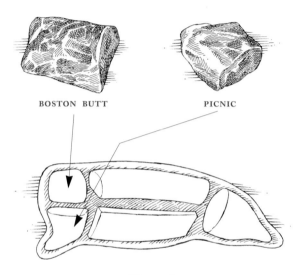

BOSTON BUTT   PICNIC

Figure 3.

*We found that pork cuts from the shoulder of the pig are best for
stewing. These cuts have enough fat (the loin, for instance, is much
too lean for stewing) to keep the meat moist as it cooks. We recommend buying a boneless Boston butt (also called a pork shoulder
blade Boston roast) or a picnic roast (also called a pork shoulder
arm picnic roast) and cutting the roast into 1½-inch cubes yourself
(see figure 5). A bone-in roast can be used but will require more
effort to prepare. You may also buy pork stew meat, but the pieces
are likely to be irregularly sized and can come from various
parts of the animal.*

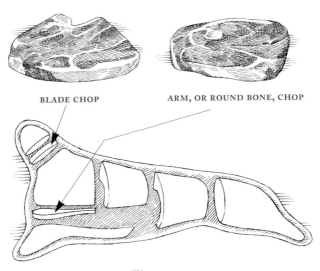

BLADE CHOP   **ARM, OR ROUND BONE, CHOP**

Figure 4.

It's very hard to find boneless lamb shoulder in markets. You might see the whole shoulder, but this cut is difficult to bone out. You can buy lamb meat for stew or, better yet, buy thick shoulder chops, remove the meat from the bone, and cut it into large cubes. There are two kinds of shoulder chops. The blade chop is roughly rectangular in shape and contains a piece of the chine bone and a thin piece of the blade bone. The arm, or round bone, chop is leaner and contains a cross-section of the arm bone. Arm chops are easier to work with, and we suggest buying about 5½ pounds of chops to yield 3 pounds of stew meat.

Figure 5.
To get stew meat pieces that are cut from the right part of the animal and regularly shaped, we suggest buying a boneless roast and cutting the meat into cubes yourself. Here, we are cutting a boneless chuck roast into 1½-inch cubes, making sure to remove excess bits of fat or gristle from each piece of meat.

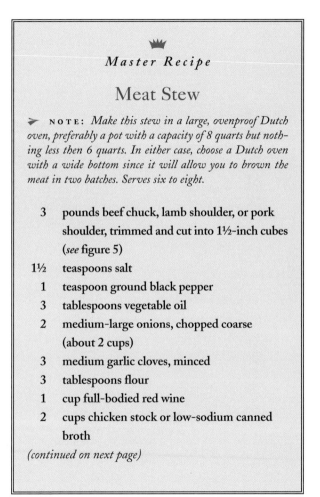

Master Recipe

Meat Stew

➤ **NOTE:** *Make this stew in a large, ovenproof Dutch oven, preferably a pot with a capacity of 8 quarts but nothing less then 6 quarts. In either case, choose a Dutch oven with a wide bottom since it will allow you to brown the meat in two batches. Serves six to eight.*

3 pounds beef chuck, lamb shoulder, or pork shoulder, trimmed and cut into 1½-inch cubes (*see* figure 5)

1½ teaspoons salt

1 teaspoon ground black pepper

3 tablespoons vegetable oil

2 medium-large onions, chopped coarse (about 2 cups)

3 medium garlic cloves, minced

3 tablespoons flour

1 cup full-bodied red wine

2 cups chicken stock or low-sodium canned broth

(continued on next page)

♥

Master Recipe
Meat Stew

(continued from previous page)

2   **bay leaves**

1   **teaspoon dried thyme**

4   **medium boiling potatoes, peeled and cut into 1-inch cubes**

4   **large carrots, peeled and sliced ¼ -inch thick**

1   **cup frozen peas (about 6 ounces), thawed**

¼   **cup minced fresh parsley leaves**

■■ INSTRUCTIONS:

1. Heat oven to 250 degrees. Place beef cubes in large bowl. Sprinkle with salt and pepper; toss to coat. Heat 2 tablespoons oil over medium-high heat in large oven-proof Dutch oven. Add half of meat and brown on all sides, about 5 minutes. Remove meat and set aside on plate. Repeat process with remaining oil and meat.

2. Add onions to empty Dutch oven and sauté until softened, 4 to 5 minutes. Add garlic and continue to cook for 30 seconds. Stir in flour and cook until lightly colored, 1 to 2 minutes. Add wine, scraping up any browned bits that may have stuck to pot. Add stock, bay leaves, and thyme, and bring to a simmer. Add meat and return to a simmer. Cover and place pot in oven. Cook for 1 hour.

3. Remove pot from oven and add potatoes and carrots. Cover and return to oven. Cook just until meat is tender, 1 to 1½ hours for lamb and 1½ to 2 hours for beef and pork. Remove pot from oven. (Can be cooled, covered, and refrigerated up to 3 days. Reheat on top of the stove.)

4. Add peas, cover, and allow to stand for 5 minutes. Stir in parsley, discard bay leaves, adjust seasonings, and serve.

Beef Stew with Bacon, Mushrooms, and Pearl Onions

➤ NOTE: *This hearty stew is our version of boeuf bourguignon. It calls for equal amounts of red wine and chicken stock. Instead of frozen pearl onions, you can use fresh pearl onions (prepared accoording to the instructions in figures 6–8, page 34). This stew is delicious over mashed potatoes. Serves six to eight.*

3	pounds beef chuck, trimmed and cut into 1½-inch cubes
1½	teaspoons salt
1	teaspoon ground black pepper
4	ounces sliced bacon, cut into ½-inch pieces
1	tablespoon vegetable oil
2	medium-large onions, chopped coarse (about 2 cups)
3	medium garlic cloves, minced
3	tablespoons flour
1½	cups full-bodied red wine
1½	cups chicken stock or low-sodium canned broth
2	bay leaves
1	teaspoon dried thyme
1	pound white button mushrooms, quartered
1	cup (8 ounces) frozen pearl onions, cooked according to package directions
¼	cup minced fresh parsley leaves

■ INSTRUCTIONS:

1. Heat oven to 250 degrees. Place beef cubes in large bowl. Sprinkle with salt and pepper; toss to coat. Fry bacon in large ovenproof Dutch oven over medium heat until golden brown, about 7 minutes. Drain bacon, reserving bits and drippings separately. Increase heat to medium-high and heat 2 tablespoons bacon drippings in Dutch oven. Add half of meat and brown on all sides, about 5 minutes. Remove meat and set aside on plate. Repeat process with another tablespoon of bacon drippings and remaining meat.

2. Add onions to empty Dutch oven and sauté until softened, 4 to 5 minutes. Add garlic and continue to cook for 30 seconds. Stir in flour and cook until lightly colored, 1 to 2 minutes. Add wine, scraping up any browned bits that may have stuck to pot. Add stock, bay leaves, and thyme, and bring to a simmer. Add meat and bacon bits return to a simmer. Cover and place pot in oven. Cook until meat is almost tender, 2 to 2½ hours.

3. Meanwhile, heat 2 tablespoons bacon drippings in large skillet. Add mushrooms and sauté over high heat until browned, 5 to 7 minutes. Transfer mushrooms to large bowl. Add cooked pearl onions and sauté until lightly browned, 2 to 3 minutes. Add onions to bowl with mushrooms.

4. Add mushrooms and onions to stew when meat is almost tender. Cover and return pot to oven. Cook until meat is completely tender, 20 to 30 minutes. (Can be cooled, covered, and refrigerated up to 3 days. Reheat on top of the stove.)

5. Stir in parsley, discard bay leaves, adjust seasonings, and serve.

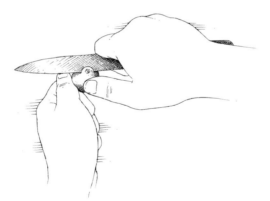

Figure 6.
To prepare fresh pearl onions, start by cutting off a tiny bit of the root end with a small paring knife.

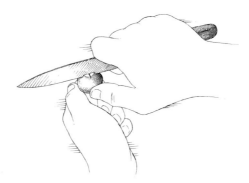

Figure 7.
To keep the onions from falling apart, cut an X in the exposed
root end of each onion. This will allow the layers to expand but
still hold together when sautéed.

Figure 8.
We find it easier to peel fresh pearl onions after they have been
blanched in boiling water for 30 seconds. Drain the onions and,
when they are cool enough to handle, simply slip off the skins.

Beef Goulash

➤ **NOTE:** *The sour cream is optional but adds a nice color and richness. Serve over egg noodles. Serves six to eight.*

3	pounds beef chuck, trimmed and cut into 1½-inch cubes
1½	teaspoons salt
1	teaspoon ground black pepper
4	ounces sliced bacon, cut into ½-inch pieces
2	medium-large onions, chopped coarse (about 2 cups)
1	medium red bell pepper, stemmed, seeded, and chopped
6	medium garlic cloves, minced
2	tablespoons sweet paprika
3	tablespoons flour
1	cup white wine
2	cups chicken stock or low-sodium canned broth
2	bay leaves
1	teaspoon dried thyme
4	large carrots, peeled and sliced ¼-inch thick
¼	cup minced fresh parsley leaves
½	cup sour cream

INSTRUCTIONS:

1. Heat oven to 250 degrees. Place beef cubes in large bowl. Sprinkle with salt and pepper; toss to coat. Fry bacon in large ovenproof Dutch oven over medium heat until golden brown, about 7 minutes. Drain bacon, reserving bits and drippings separately. Increase heat to medium-high and heat 2 tablespoons bacon drippings in Dutch oven. Add half of meat and brown on all sides, about 5 minutes. Remove meat and set aside on plate. Repeat process with another tablespoon of bacon drippings and remaining meat.

2. Add onions and red bell pepper to empty Dutch oven and sauté until softened, 4 to 5 minutes. Add garlic and continue to cook for 30 seconds. Stir in paprika and flour; cook 1 to 2 minutes. Add wine, scraping up any browned bits that may have stuck to pot. Add stock, bay leaves, and thyme, and bring to a simmer. Add meat and return to a simmer. Cover and place pot in oven. Cook for 1 hour.

3. Remove pot from oven and add carrots. Cover and return to oven. Cook just until meat is tender, 1½ to 2 hours. Remove pot from oven. (Can be cooled, covered, and refrigerated up to 3 days. Reheat on top of the stove.)

4. Stir in parsley and sour cream, discard bay leaves, adjust seasonings, and serve. Once sour cream has been added, do not let stew simmer or boil or sour cream will curdle.

Belgian Beef Stew with Beer

➤ **NOTE**: *This famed Belgian stew, called carbonnade, uses beer for the cooking liquid. We found that an amber-colored ale, such as Pete's Wicked Ale or Anchor Steam Ale, gave the stew the richest flavor without any harshness. Traditionally, carbonnade contains just beef, onions, and beer for an intensely flavored stew. We found that brown sugar mellows the flavor of the beer, vinegar sharpens the other flavors, and mustard gives the broth some spice. The stew is delicious served over egg noodles. Since this stew does not contain any root vegetables, it can also be served over mashed potatoes or any root vegetable puree. Serves six to eight.*

3	pounds beef chuck, trimmed and cut into 1½-inch cubes
1½	teaspoons salt
1	teaspoon ground black pepper
3	tablespoons vegetable oil
2	pounds onions, thinly sliced
2	medium garlic cloves, minced
3	tablespoons flour
1½	cups amber-colored ale
1½	cups chicken stock or low-sodium canned broth
2	bay leaves
1	teaspoon dried thyme
1	tablespoon brown sugar
1	tablespoon cider vinegar
1	tablespoon Dijon mustard
¼	cup minced fresh parsley leaves

:: INSTRUCTIONS:

1. Heat oven to 250 degrees. Place beef cubes in large bowl. Sprinkle with salt and pepper; toss to coat. Heat 2 tablespoons oil over medium-high heat in large ovenproof Dutch oven. Add half of beef and brown on all sides, about 5 minutes. Remove meat and set aside on plate. Repeat process with remaining oil and beef.

2. Add onions to empty Dutch oven and sauté, stirring frequently until onions release their liquid and in essence deglaze the pan, 10 to 12 minutes. Reduce heat to medium; cook until liquid evaporates, drippings begin to brown, and onions become quite dark, about 15 to 20 minutes. Add garlic and continue to cook for 30 seconds. Stir in flour and cook until lightly colored, 1 to 2 minutes. Add ale, scraping up any browned bits that may have stuck to pot. Add stock, bay leaves, thyme, brown sugar, and vinegar, and bring to a simmer. Add meat and return to a simmer. Cover and place pot in oven. Cook just until meat is tender, 2 to 2½ hours. Remove pot from oven. (Can be cooled, covered, and refrigerated up to 3 days. Reheat on top of the stove.)

3. Stir in mustard and parsley, discard bay leaves, adjust seasonings, and serve.

Irish Stew

➤ **NOTE:** *Lamb stew is a favorite dish in Ireland. The broth is made with all stock (no wine), and potatoes and carrots are the most typical vegetables. Without the wine, the stew liquid is particularly meaty. Adding a little Worcestershire sauce intensifies the meatiness of the stew. Serves six to eight.*

3	pounds lamb shoulder, trimmed and cut into 1½-inch cubes
1½	teaspoons salt
1	teaspoon ground black pepper
3	tablespoons vegetable oil
3	medium-large onions, chopped coarse (about 3 cups)
3	tablespoons flour
3	cups chicken stock or low-sodium canned broth
½	teaspoon Worcestershire sauce
2	bay leaves
1	teaspoon dried thyme
6	medium boiling potatoes, peeled and cut into 1-inch dice
4	large carrots, peeled and sliced ¼-inch thick
¼	cup minced fresh parsley leaves

■■ INSTRUCTIONS:

1. Heat oven to 250 degrees. Place lamb cubes in large bowl. Sprinkle with salt and pepper; toss to coat. Heat 2 tablespoons oil over medium-high heat in large ovenproof Dutch oven. Add half of lamb and brown on all sides, about 5 minutes. Remove meat and set aside on plate. Repeat process with remaining oil and lamb.

2. Add onions to empty Dutch oven and sauté until softened, 4 to 5 minutes. Stir in flour and cook until lightly colored, 1 to 2 minutes. Add 1 cup stock, scraping up any browned bits that may have stuck to pot. Add remaining stock, Worcestershire sauce, bay leaves, and thyme, and bring to a simmer. Add meat and return to a simmer. Cover and place pot in oven. Cook for 1 hour.

3. Remove pot from oven and add potatoes and carrots. Cover and return to oven. Cook just until meat is tender, 1 to 1½ hours. Remove pot from oven. (Can be cooled, covered, and refrigerated up to 3 days. Reheat on top of the stove.)

4. Stir in parsley, discard bay leaves, adjust seasonings, and serve.

Lamb Stew with Tomatoes, Chickpeas, and Spices

➤ NOTE: *In this North African stew, canned tomatoes take the place of the wine. Because no vegetables are added partway through the cooking process, the total stewing time for the lamb is reduced to about 2 hours. Serve this stew over couscous. Serves six to eight.*

3	pounds lamb shoulder, trimmed and cut into 1½-inch cubes
1½	teaspoons salt
1	teaspoon ground black pepper
3	tablespoons vegetable oil
2	medium-large onions, chopped coarse (about 2 cups)
4	medium garlic cloves, minced
3	tablespoons flour
1½	cups chicken stock or low-sodium canned broth
1½	cups chopped canned tomatoes with their juice
2	bay leaves
1½	teaspoons ground coriander
1	teaspoon ground cumin
¾	teaspoon ground cinnamon
½	teaspoon ground ginger
1	15-ounce can chickpeas, drained and rinsed
¼	cup minced fresh parsley or cilantro leaves

:: INSTRUCTIONS:

1. Heat oven to 250 degrees. Place lamb cubes in large bowl. Sprinkle with salt and pepper; toss to coat. Heat 2 tablespoons oil over medium-high heat in large ovenproof Dutch oven. Add half of lamb and brown on all sides, about 5 minutes. Remove meat and set aside on plate. Repeat process with remaining oil and lamb.

2. Add onions to empty Dutch oven and sauté until softened, 4 to 5 minutes. Add garlic and continue to cook for 30 seconds. Stir in flour and cook until lightly colored, 1 to 2 minutes. Add stock, scraping up any browned bits that may have stuck to pot. Add tomatoes, coriander, cumin, cinnamon, ginger, and bay leaves, and bring to a simmer. Add meat and return to a simmer. Cover and place pot in oven. Cook just until meat is almost tender, 1¾ to 2¼ hours.

3. Remove pot from oven and add chickpeas. Cover and return pot to oven and cook until meat is tender and chickpeas are heated through, about 15 minutes. (Can be cooled, covered, and refrigerated up to 3 days. Reheat on top of the stove.)

4. Stir in parsley, discard bay leaves, adjust seasonings, and serve.

Lamb Stew with Rosemary and White Beans

➤ NOTE: *In this Italian stew, cannellini or other white beans take the place of the potatoes. Rosemary is used in place of the thyme. Since this dish contains beans, it can be served as is, or perhaps with some bread, but it does not require any other starch. Serves six to eight.*

3	pounds lamb shoulder, trimmed and cut into 1½-inch cubes
1½	teaspoons salt
1	teaspoon ground black pepper
3	tablespoons vegetable oil
2	medium-large onions, chopped coarse (about 2 cups)
3	medium garlic cloves, minced
3	tablespoons flour
1	cup white wine
2	cups chicken stock or low-sodium canned broth
2	bay leaves
1	tablespoon minced fresh rosemary
3	large carrots, peeled and cut into ⅜-inch dice
1	15-ounce can white beans, drained and rinsed
¼	cup minced fresh parsley leaves

INSTRUCTIONS:

1. Heat oven to 250 degrees. Place lamb cubes in large bowl. Sprinkle with salt and pepper; toss to coat. Heat 2 tablespoons oil over medium-high heat in large ovenproof Dutch oven. Add half of lamb and brown on all sides, about 5 minutes. Remove meat and set aside on plate. Repeat process with remaining oil and lamb.

2. Add onions to empty Dutch oven and sauté until softened, 4 to 5 minutes. Add garlic and continue to cook for 30 seconds. Stir in flour and cook until lightly colored, 1 to 2 minutes. Add wine, scraping up any browned bits that may have stuck to pot. Add stock, bay leaves, and rosemary, and bring to a simmer. Add meat and return to a simmer. Cover and place pot in oven. Cook for 1 hour.

3. Remove pot from oven and add carrots. Cover and return to oven. Cook just until meat is almost tender, 1 to 1¼ hours. Remove pot from oven and add white beans. Cover and return pot to oven and cook until meat is tender and beans are heated through, about 15 minutes. Remove pot from oven. (Can be cooled, covered, and refrigerated up to 3 days. Reheat on top of the stove.)

4. Stir in parsley, discard bay leaves, adjust seasonings, and serve.

Pork Stew with Prunes, Mustard, and Cream

➤ **NOTE:** *This French stew features prunes soaked in brandy. The liquid is enriched with cream. If you like, use Armagnac in place of the brandy. Ladle this stew over buttered noodles. Serves six to eight.*

6	ounces prunes, halved and soaked in ⅓ cup brandy, until softened, about 20 minutes
3	pounds pork shoulder, trimmed and cut into 1 ½-inch cubes
1½	teaspoons salt
1	teaspoon ground black pepper
3	tablespoons vegetable oil
2	medium-large onions, chopped coarse (about 2 cups)
3	medium garlic cloves, minced
3	tablespoons flour
1	cup white wine
2	cups chicken stock or low-sodium canned broth
2	bay leaves
1	teaspoon dried thyme
½	cup heavy cream
3	tablespoons Dijon mustard
¼	cup minced fresh parsley leaves

■ INSTRUCTIONS:

1. Heat oven to 250 degrees. Place pork cubes in large bowl. Sprinkle with salt and pepper; toss to coat. Heat 2 tablespoons oil over medium-high heat in large ovenproof Dutch oven. Add half of pork and brown on all sides, about 5 minutes. Remove meat and set aside on plate. Repeat process with remaining oil and pork.

2. Add onions to empty Dutch oven and sauté until softened, 4 to 5 minutes. Add garlic and continue to cook for 30 seconds. Stir in flour and cook until lightly colored, 1 to 2 minutes. Add wine, scraping up any browned bits that may have stuck to pot. Add stock, bay leaves, and thyme, and bring to a simmer. Add meat and return to a simmer. Cover and place pot in oven. Cook for 2 hours.

3. Add prunes, brandy, and cream. Cover and return to oven. Cook just until meat is tender, 30 to 45 minutes. Remove pot from oven. (Can be cooled, covered, and refrigerated up to 3 days. Reheat on top of the stove.)

4. Stir in mustard and parsley, discard bay leaves, adjust seasonings, and serve.

Pork Vindaloo

➤ **NOTE:** *This Indian dish of Portuguese ancestry relies on tomatoes instead of wine as part of the liquid base. Pair this stew with steamed rice, preferably basmati rice. Serves six to eight.*

3	pounds pork shoulder, trimmed and cut into 1½-inch cubes
1½	teaspoons salt
1	teaspoon ground black pepper
3	tablespoons vegetable oil
3	medium-large onions, chopped coarse (about 3 cups)
8	medium garlic cloves, minced
3	tablespoons flour
1	tablespoon sweet paprika
¾	teaspoon ground cumin
½	teaspoon ground cardamom
¼	teaspoon cayenne
¼	teaspoon ground cloves
1½	cups chicken stock or low-sodium canned broth
1½	cups chopped canned tomatoes with their juice
2	bay leaves
1	teaspoon sugar
2	tablespoons red wine vinegar
1	tablespoon mustard seeds
¼	cup minced fresh cilantro leaves

4 8

■ INSTRUCTIONS:

1. Heat oven to 250 degrees. Place pork cubes in large bowl. Sprinkle with salt and pepper; toss to coat. Heat 2 tablespoons oil over medium-high heat in large ovenproof Dutch oven. Add half of pork and brown on all sides, about 5 minutes. Remove meat and set aside on plate. Repeat process with remaining oil and pork.

2. Add onions to empty Dutch oven and sauté until softened, 4 to 5 minutes. Add garlic and continue to cook for 30 seconds. Stir in flour, paprika, cumin, cardamom, cayenne, and cloves, and cook until lightly colored, 1 to 2 minutes. Add stock, scraping up any browned bits that may have stuck to pot. Add tomatoes, bay leaves, sugar, vinegar, and mustard seeds, and bring to a simmer. Add meat and return to a simmer. Cover and place pot in oven. Cook just until meat is tender, about 2½ hours. Remove pot from oven. (Can be cooled, covered, and refrigerated up to 3 days. Reheat on top of the stove.)

3. Stir in cilantro, discard bay leaves, adjust seasonings, and serve.

chapter three

CHICKEN STEWS

CHICKEN STEW IS A BIT HARD TO DEFINE. Say beef stew and most everyone can imagine large, boneless chunks of browned beef floating in a rich, dark sauce along with some vegetables. But what exactly is chicken stew? Is it a cut-up chicken that is browned and then braised? Is it a cut-up chicken that is stewed (to make homemade broth) and then cooled in order to tear the meat from the bones? Is it boneless breasts or thighs cut into chunks and browned and stewed like beef?

We started with a whole chicken that was cut up, browned, and then simmered in water to make stock. The liquid was strained and the meat was removed from the breasts, legs, and thighs. Like meat stew, this preparation produced a stew without bones, and the homemade stock was a nice bonus. But the dish required a lot of effort (pulling the meat off each piece is very tedious) and the results were good but not great.

Our next thought was to follow our master recipe for meat stew but use a cut-up chicken instead of cubes of boneless beef, lamb, or pork. We browned the chicken parts, removed them from the pot, sautéed some aromatic vegetables, deglazed the pot with some wine, added stock, slow-cooking vegetables, and the chicken, and simmered until everything was tender. We encountered several problems with this method. The skin is nice and crisp after browning but becomes flabby and not very appealing after stewing in liquid for the necessary half hour or so. In addition, the wings are very unappetizing—they contain mostly inedible skin and very little meat. Also, the breast pieces were way too large to fit into a bowl (each piece would have to be cut in half crosswise) and they had dried out during the stewing process.

We tried this recipe again using just breasts and legs. We cut the split breasts in half, browned all the parts, pulled off the skin, and then added the legs to the stew followed by the breasts. Although the breasts were less dry and stringy, we felt that the dark meat pieces, with their extra fat and connective tissue, were better suited to stewing. They had much more flavor and their texture was more appealing. In addition, our tasters preferred the meatier thighs to the drumsticks, which tend to have more bone. The thighs are also easier to eat than the drumsticks, with the meat easily separating from the bones. We decided to abandon the breasts and drumsticks and concentrate on a stew made with thighs only.

This last test had revealed something interesting about the thighs. Removing the skin after the parts were browned was a must. The stew liquid was much less fatty, and since the skin was very soft and flabby and not really edible, there seemed little reason to serve it to people. We wondered if we should just start with boneless, skinless thighs—it certainly would be easier to eat a stew without bones. Unfortunately, when we browned boneless, skinless thighs, the outer layer of meat became tough and dry. Also, the skinless thighs tended to stick to the pan, even when we added quite a bit of oil. The skin acts as a cushion between the meat and pan.

We had decided on the style of chicken stew and for the most part liked the master recipe for meat stew adapted to chicken. But we found that we could not simply take the meat stew recipe wholesale and just add chicken instead of beef, lamb, or pork.

First of all, meat stews often taste best with red wine.

Chicken generally matches up better with white wine. Also, because chicken requires less cooking time, we found that a stew made with one cup of wine and two cups of stock (as suggested in our meat stew recipes) was too alcoholic. Cutting the wine back to half a cup and increasing the stock by a half a cup keeps the stew from being too boozy. We also found that chicken's milder flavor calls for less aggressive seasoning. Therefore, we used one less bay leaf and half as much thyme as in our meat stew recipe.

Like meat stew, chicken stew responds best to subboiling temperatures, which are easier to maintain in a low oven. However, when we put the chicken in a 250-degree oven it took almost the entire cooking time for the liquid to come up to temperature. We raised the oven temperature to 300 degrees and found that the stew was ready 30 minutes after the chicken was added to the liquid. Although this higher temperature would eventually cause the stew temperature to rise to the boiling point, we found that the temperature was just about 200 degrees when the chicken was done.

Because chicken requires so much less time to cook than meat, vegetables are added before the chicken, not after. For instance, the carrots and potatoes get a 10-minute head start on the chicken so that they will be tender by the time the chicken is cooked through.

Master Recipe

Chicken Stew

➤ NOTE: *We recommend using regular chicken thighs in this recipe. As a second option, you may use boneless, skinless chicken thighs, although the outer layer of meat will toughen during the cooking process. Substitute boneless, skinless thighs and sauté them in batches, adding a few more tablespoons of vegetable oil during the process to keep them from sticking. You may need to use a metal spatula to loosen browned skinless thighs from the pan. Serves six to eight.*

8	bone-in, skin-on chicken thighs (about 3 pounds)
½	teaspoon salt
¼	teaspoon ground black pepper
2	tablespoons vegetable oil
1	large onion, chopped coarse
2	medium garlic cloves, minced
3	tablespoons flour
½	cup white wine
2½	cups chicken stock or low-sodium canned broth
1	bay leaf

½	teaspoon dried thyme
4	large carrots, peeled and sliced ¼-inch thick
4	medium boiling potatoes, peeled and cut into ½-inch cubes
1	cup frozen peas (about 6 ounces), thawed
¼	cup minced fresh parsley leaves

INSTRUCTIONS:

1. Heat oven to 300 degrees. Sprinkle chicken with salt and pepper. Heat oil over medium-high heat in large ovenproof Dutch oven. Add half of chicken, skin side down, and brown, about 4 minutes. Turn chicken and brown on other side, about 4 minutes. Remove chicken and set aside on plate. Repeat process with remaining chicken. Drain and discard all but 1 tablespoon fat from pot. When chicken has cooled, remove and discard skin (*see* figure 9).

2. Add onion to empty Dutch oven and sauté until softened, 4 to 5 minutes. Add garlic and continue to cook for 30 seconds. Stir in flour and cook until lightly colored, 1 to 2 minutes. Add wine, scraping up any browned bits that may have stuck to pot. Add stock, bay leaf, and thyme, and bring to a simmer. Add carrots and potatoes and simmer for 10 minutes. Add chicken, submerging it in liquid, and return to a simmer. Cover and place pot in oven. Cook for 30 minutes. Remove pot from oven. (Can be cooled, covered, and refrigerated up to 3 days. Reheat on top of the stove.)

3. Add peas, cover, and let to stand for 5 minutes. Stir in parsley, discard bay leaf, adjust seasonings, and serve.

Figure 9
Once the chicken thighs have been browned and cooled, grasp the skin from one end and pull to separate the skin from the meat. Discard the skin.

Chicken Stew with Leeks, Potatoes, and Saffron

➤ NOTE: *Saffron gives this stew a yellow-orange hue and a rich, earthy flavor. Buy saffron threads (not powder) and crumble them yourself for the best flavor. Serves six to eight.*

8	bone-in, skin-on chicken thighs (about 3 pounds)
½	teaspoon salt
¼	teaspoon ground black pepper
2	tablespoons vegetable oil
4	large leeks, light green and white parts, sliced thin
2	medium garlic cloves, minced
3	tablespoons flour
½	cup white wine
2½	cups chicken stock or low-sodium canned broth
1	bay leaf
½	teaspoon dried thyme
¼	teaspoon saffron threads
4	large carrots, peeled and sliced ¼-inch thick
4	medium boiling potatoes, cut into ½-inch cubes
¼	cup minced fresh parsley leaves

▋ INSTRUCTIONS:

1. Heat oven to 300 degrees. Sprinkle chicken with salt and pepper. Heat oil over medium-high heat in large ovenproof

Dutch oven. Add half of chicken, skin side down, and brown, about 4 minutes. Turn chicken and brown on other side, about 4 minutes. Remove chicken and set aside on plate. Repeat process with remaining chicken. Drain and discard all but 1 tablespoon fat from pot. When chicken has cooled, remove and discard skin.

2. Add leeks to empty Dutch oven and sauté until softened, 4 to 5 minutes. Add garlic and continue to cook for 30 seconds. Stir in flour and cook until lightly colored, 1 to 2 minutes. Add wine, scraping up any browned bits that may have stuck to pot. Add stock, bay leaf, and thyme, and bring to a simmer. Crumble saffron threads between fingers right over pot to release flavor (*see* figure 10). Add carrots and potatoes and simmer for 10 minutes. Add chicken, submerging it in liquid, and return to a simmer. Cover and place pot in oven. Cook for 30 minutes. Remove pot from oven. (Can be cooled, covered, and refrigerated up to 3 days. Reheat on top of the stove.)

3. Stir in parsley, discard bay leaf, adjust seasonings, and serve.

Figure 10.
To release their flavor, crumble saffron threads between your
fingers right over the pot.

Country Captain Chicken Stew

➤ NOTE: *A Southern favorite. We like this curried chicken stew with fresh mangoes rather than the usual mango chutney. Rice is a good accompaniment to this stew. Serves six to eight.*

8	bone-in, skin-on chicken thighs (about 3 pounds)
½	teaspoon salt
¼	teaspoon ground black pepper
2	tablespoons vegetable oil
2	large onions, chopped coarse
1	green bell pepper, stemmed, seeded, and chopped
2	medium garlic cloves, minced
1½	tablespoons sweet paprika
1	tablespoon curry powder
¼	teaspoon cayenne pepper
3	tablespoons flour
1½	cups chicken stock or low-sodium canned broth
1½	cups chopped canned tomatoes with their juice
1	bay leaf
½	teaspoon dried thyme
½	cup raisins
1	ripe mango, peeled, pitted, and cut into ¼-inch dice
¼	cup minced fresh parsley leaves

:: INSTRUCTIONS:

1. Heat oven to 300 degrees. Sprinkle chicken with salt and pepper. Heat oil over medium-high heat in large ovenproof Dutch oven. Add half of chicken, skin side down, and brown, about 4 minutes. Turn chicken and brown on other side, about 4 minutes. Remove chicken and set aside on plate. Repeat process with remaining chicken. Drain and discard all but 1 tablespoon fat from pot. When chicken has cooled, remove and discard skin.

2. Add onions and bell pepper to empty Dutch oven and sauté until softened, 4 to 5 minutes. Add garlic and continue to cook for 30 seconds. Stir in paprika, curry powder, and cayenne and cook until spices are fragrant, about 30 seconds. Stir in flour and cook 1 to 2 minutes. Add stock, scraping up any browned bits that may have stuck to pot. Add tomatoes, bay leaf, thyme, raisins, and mango, and bring to a simmer. Simmer for 10 minutes to blend flavors. Add chicken, submerging it in liquid, and return to a simmer. Cover and place pot in oven. Cook for 30 minutes. Remove pot from oven. (Can be cooled, covered, and refrigerated up to 3 days. Reheat on top of the stove.)

3. Stir in parsley, discard bay leaf, adjust seasonings, and serve.

chapter four

ℨ

SEAFOOD STEWS

IND A COUNTRY THAT HAS A COASTLINE, AND you will find a fish stew in the culinary reper- toire. Whatever their geographic origin, fish stews are surprisingly easy for home cooks to prepare. Most recipes begin by making stock. The next step is to make a flavor base. The stock is added and then the fish.

Although the process is straightforward, we had a num- ber of questions. Is fish stock essential? If so, what kinds of fish make the best stock? What ingredients are essential in the flavor base and which are optional? What kinds of fish respond best to stewing? What size should the pieces of fish be? How long should they cook?

We started our testing by making a favorite fish stew with homemade fish stock, water, chicken stock, and a

6 2

"cheater's" stock that started with bottled clam juice. The stew made with homemade fish stock was far superior. Unlike meat or chicken stews, where the protein simmers for some time in the stew, fish can cook for only a few minutes or it will dry out and fall apart. Since the fish does not have time to flavor the stew liquid, the liquid must start out tasting good. Water made a horrible fish stew. Chicken stock tasted too much like chicken. Bottled clam juice, doctored up with some fresh ingredients, is our second choice if making fish stock is impossible.

We tested various fish for making stock and preferred those with heads and bones that will produce a gelatinous stock. (*See* page 66 for more details.) Trimmings can come from any number of fish, although oily, strong-tasting fish, such as bluefish or salmon, should be avoided.

Many recipes suggest sweating fish bones and vegetables before adding water to make stock. In our tests, we found that this step was not only unnecessary but also yielded an inferior stock. We found that simply adding all the ingredients to the pot, including the water, at the same time, produces a cleaner, brighter tasting stock.

Unlike meat or chicken stock, fish stock is rarely simmered for hours. Some sources warn against simmering for longer than 15 or 30 minutes, suggesting that the trimmings will make the stock bitter if cooked too long. We tested various times and found that fish stock tastes best when simmered for a full hour. When we continued to simmer the stock for another hour there was no improvement in flavor, but the stock did not become bitter, either.

There was a time when fishmongers would gladly give away bones, heads, and tails. But no longer, unless perhaps you are an especially good customer. And don't expect to automatically have bones available when you show up. Call ahead and reserve what you need.

In addition to fish trimmings, water, and aromatic vegetables, many recipes call for white wine. We made fish stock both with and without wine and found that the wine adds a pleasant acidity. (Adding a little lemon adds some acidity, but not enough. We found that adding more than a quarter of a lemon will make the stock taste overly lemony.)

The prime flavoring element for many fish stews is a seasoned tomato sauce, or base. Like stock, aromatic vegetables (onions, carrots, and celery) add flavor. However, for the base these vegetables should be sautéed to bring out their full flavor. Again, white wine brings a much-needed acidic edge to the stew. Other ingredients, such as fresh fennel and Pernod for bouillabaisse or almonds and red bell pepper for zarzuela, are added to give specific stews their character. Whatever the ingredients, the base should be well seasoned; it will be diluted with fish stock, which is cooked without salt.

We tested bases made with fresh and canned tomatoes. We found little difference, so don't hesitate to use canned tomatoes. Unlike the stock, the base for the stew doesn't improve with longer cooking. After twenty minutes, the tomatoes begin to lose their freshness. After thirty minutes, the tomato base tastes too acidic and all the fresh tomato flavor is gone. Once the tomatoes are added, we recommend simmering the stew base just long enough to thicken the consistency and blend flavors, 15 to 20 minutes.

Once the base is cooked, it's time to add the stock and bring the mixture to a boil. The fish is then added and cooked briefly. In our testing, we found that overcooking the fish is the biggest problem with most fish stews. We found that 3- to 4-ounce pieces are best for serving (they are neither too large to eat gracefully nor so small that they fall apart in the stew). Pieces of fish this small, however, cook very quickly. We tried various simmering and boiling regimens. In the end, what worked best was cooking the fish in simmering broth for 5 minutes, followed by 5 minutes of indirect cooking with the heat turned off and the lid on the pot.

Any white-fleshed fillet can be used in fish stew. In general, we like firmer fillets, such as red snapper or monkfish. Tender fillets, such as flounder or sole, can be used, but you might want to reduce the simmering time by a minute or two to keep these thinner fillets from overcooking.

CHOOSING FISH FOR STOCK

Several kinds of fish make an exceptionally good stock that is rich and gelatinous. These fish are listed in the first grouping and should be used when possible. Most other tender white fish are fine for stock as well, and these are listed in the second grouping. Avoid the oily fish in the third grouping when making stock.

■■ BEST FISH FOR STOCK

Blackfish
Monkfish, especially the heads
Red snapper
Sea bass

■■ COMMON FISH THAT MAKE GOOD STOCK

Cod
Flatfish (sole, flounder, etc.)
Haddock
Pacific pollack
Rockfish
Shells from lobster, shrimp, or crabs
Skate

■■ FISH TO AVOID

Bluefish
Mackerel
Pompano

Salmon
Smelt

Fish Stock

➤ NOTE: *Fish heads, tails, and bones can be used to make stock. An equal amount of lobster, shrimp, or crab shells may be used instead. Makes 2 to 2½ quarts.*

3	pounds fish trimmings (*see* page 66), prepared according to figures 11–13
1	medium onion, diced
2	medium carrots, diced
1	large celery stalk, diced
8	fresh parsley stems, chopped
1	cup dry white wine
1	lemon quarter
10	whole black peppercorns
2	bay leaves
1	dried chile pepper

▚ INSTRUCTIONS:

1. Put all ingredients in 6- to 8-quart pot. Cover with 2¾ quarts cold water. Bring to boil over medium heat; simmer gently for 1 hour, periodically skimming away scum that rises to surface.

2. Strain stock through double thickness of cheesecloth, pressing out as much liquid as possible with back of spoon. (Stock can be cooled and refrigerated for up to 3 days or frozen for 3 months.)

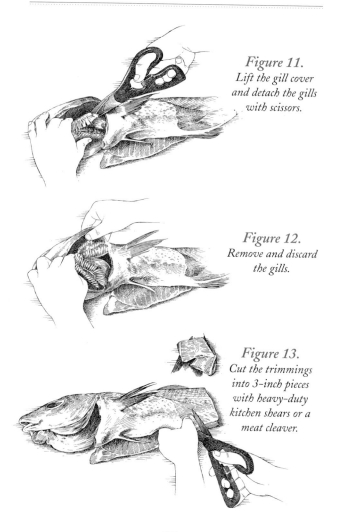

Figure 11.
Lift the gill cover and detach the gills with scissors.

Figure 12.
Remove and discard the gills.

Figure 13.
Cut the trimmings into 3-inch pieces with heavy-duty kitchen shears or a meat cleaver.

Cheater's Fish Stock

➤ NOTE: *We found that doctored clam juice can be used in a pinch in place of fish stock. Clam juice is very salty, so don't add any salt to the stew until you have tasted it. Makes about 4½ cups.*

1	small onion, minced
1	medium carrot, minced
2	medium celery stalks, minced
8	fresh parsley stems, chopped
1	cup dry white wine
3	8-ounce bottles clam juice
3	cups water
2	bay leaves
8	whole black peppercorns
½	teaspoon dried thyme
1	tablespoon lemon juice
1	dried chile pepper

∷ INSTRUCTIONS:

Bring all ingredients to boil in medium saucepan. Simmer to blend flavors (no skimming necessary), about 30 minutes. Strain through cheesecloth, pressing on solids with back of spoon to extract as much liquid as possible. (Can be refrigerated for 3 days.)

♛

Master Recipe

Fish Stew

➤ NOTE: *Red snapper, cod, grouper, monkfish, and sea bass are our favorite choices for stew. However, any white-fleshed fillet can be used either singly or in combination with another kind of fish. Because fish stew does not involve browning of meat and the stew does not go into the oven, it is not necessary to use a Dutch oven. A regular soup pot works just fine, although you may use a Dutch oven if you prefer. Serves six to eight.*

2	tablespoons olive oil
1	medium onion, diced
1	medium celery stalk, diced
1	medium carrot, diced
3	large garlic cloves, minced
½	cup dry white wine
2	cups chopped canned tomatoes with juice
2	large bay leaves
⅛	teaspoon cayenne pepper, or to taste
	Salt and ground black pepper
4½	cups Fish Stock (page 67) or Cheater's Fish Stock (page 69)

3   pounds white-flesh fish fillets, rinsed, patted
     dry, and cut into 3- to 4-ounce pieces
¼   cup minced fresh parsley leaves

INSTRUCTIONS:

1. Heat oil in large soup kettle. Add onion, celery, carrot, and garlic and cook over medium heat until softened, about 10 minutes. Add wine and simmer until reduced by half, 2 to 3 minutes. Add tomatoes, bay leaves, cayenne pepper, and salt and pepper to taste. Bring to boil, reduce heat, and simmer until mixture has thickened to tomato sauce consistency, 15 to 20 minutes.

2. Add fish stock and bring to boil. Reduce heat to simmer and adjust seasonings with salt, pepper, and cayenne to taste.

3. Add fish pieces and simmer, stirring a few times to ensure even cooking, for 5 minutes. Remove kettle from heat, cover, and let stand until fish is just cooked through, about 5 minutes. Stir in parsley, discard bay leaves, and serve immediately.

Cod Stew with Potatoes and Bacon

➤ **N O T E :** *This simple New England–style fish stew contains just cod, potatoes, onions, and bacon. Other firm, white-fleshed fish fillets may be used, but cod is the most authentic choice. The stew is delicious as is but can be enriched with a little heavy cream just before serving if you like. Serves six to eight.*

4	ounces sliced bacon, cut into ¼-inch pieces
1	medium onion, diced
½	cup dry white wine
2	cups chopped canned tomatoes with their juice
2	large bay leaves
⅛	teaspoon cayenne pepper, or to taste
	Salt and ground black pepper
4½	cups Fish Stock (page 67) or Cheater's Fish Stock (page 69)
3	medium boiling potatoes, cut into ½-inch cubes
½	cup heavy cream (optional)
3	pounds cod fillets, rinsed, patted dry, and cut into 3- to 4-ounce pieces
¼	cup minced fresh parsley leaves

⠿ **I N S T R U C T I O N S :**

1. Fry bacon in large soup kettle over medium heat until nicely browned, about 7 minutes. Remove bacon with slotted spoon and set aside. Add onion to bacon fat and cook over medium heat until softened, about 10 minutes. Add wine and simmer until reduced by half, 2 to 3 minutes. Add tomatoes, bay leaves, cayenne pepper, and salt and pepper to taste. Bring to boil, reduce heat, and simmer until mixture has thickened to tomato sauce consistency, 15 to 20 minutes.

2. Add fish stock and potatoes and bring to boil. Reduce heat and simmer until potatoes are almost tender, 10 to 15 minutes. Add cream, if using. Adjust seasonings with salt, pepper, and cayenne to taste.

3. Add fish pieces and simmer, stirring a few times to ensure even cooking, for 5 minutes. Remove kettle from heat, cover, and let stand until fish is just cooked through, about 5 minutes. Stir in bacon and parsley, discard bay leaves, and serve immediately.

Bouillabaisse

➤ NOTE: *This French fish stew is served in soup plates that have been lined with sliced cooked potatoes. Float two slices of toasted French bread dolloped with Roasted Red Pepper Mayonnaise (see recipe on page 76) in each bowl. Serves eight.*

2	tablespoons olive oil
2	medium onions, diced
1	small fennel bulb, diced, tough parts and stalks discarded
6	large garlic cloves, minced
½	cup dry white wine
3	cups chopped canned tomatoes with their juice
¼	teaspoon saffron threads, crumbled (*see* figure 10, page 59)
3	tablespoons anise-flavored liqueur such as Pernod
1	teaspoon grated orange zest
2	large bay leaves
⅛	teaspoon cayenne pepper, or to taste
	Salt and ground black pepper
4½	cups Fish Stock (page 67) or Cheater's Fish Stock (page 69)
1	pound new potatoes
3	pounds white-flesh fish fillets, rinsed, patted dry, and cut into 3- to 4-ounce pieces
1	recipe Roasted Red Pepper Mayonnaise

16   slices ½-inch-thick French bread, toasted

¼   cup minced fresh parsley leaves

⁝⁝ I N S T R U C T I O N S :

1. Heat oil in large soup kettle. Add onions, fennel, and garlic and cook over medium heat until softened, about 10 minutes. Add wine and simmer until reduced by half, 2 to 3 minutes. Add tomatoes, saffron, Pernod, orange zest, bay leaves, cayenne pepper, and salt and pepper to taste. Bring to boil, reduce heat, and simmer until mixture has thickened to tomato sauce consistency, 15 to 20 minutes.

2. Add fish stock and bring to boil. Reduce heat to simmer and adjust seasonings with salt, pepper, and cayenne to taste.

3. Meanwhile, place potatoes in medium saucepan and cover with water. Bring to boil and simmer until cooked through, 15 to 20 minutes. Drain, cool slightly, and cut into thick slices. Cover and keep potatoes warm.

4. Add fish to stew and simmer, stirring a few times, for 5 minutes. Remove kettle from heat, cover, and let stand until fish is just cooked through, about 5 minutes.

5. Spread a dollop of mayonnaise over each piece of toast. Divide potato slices among soup plates. Stir parsley into stew, discard bay leaves, and ladle stew into soup plates. Float 2 toasts in each soup plate and serve immediately.

Roasted Red Pepper Mayonnaise

➤ NOTE: *Spread this French sauce, called rouille, on toasts that you float in bowls of seafood stew. If you like, mix the mayonnaise right into the stew for added flavor. If you prefer not to eat dishes with raw eggs, replace the egg yolk and olive oil with ¾ cup prepared mayonnaise, adding the mayonnaise with the pepper and saffron and processing until smooth. Makes about 1 cup.*

- 2   large garlic cloves, peeled
- 1   slice (about ½-inch-thick) French bread
- 1   small red bell pepper, roasted, peeled, and seeded
- ⅛   teaspoon saffron threads, crumbled (*see* figure 10, page 59)
- 1   large egg yolk, at room temperature
- ½   cup olive oil

    Salt

    Pinch cayenne pepper

⊞ INSTRUCTIONS:

With food processor motor running, drop garlic cloves, one at a time, through feed tube. Push garlic down sides of bowl with rubber spatula. Add bread and process to fine crumbs. Add bell pepper, saffron, then egg yolk and process until pureed. With motor still running, slowly add oil until mixture thickens to mayonnaise consistency. Season to taste with salt and cayenne pepper.

Sicilian Fish Stew

➤ NOTE: *Serve this heady stew with bruschetta—slices of country-style Italian bread that have been toasted, rubbed with a cut garlic clove, and brushed with olive oil. Serves six to eight.*

2	tablespoons olive oil
2	medium onions, diced
3	large garlic cloves, minced
½	cup dry white wine
2	cups chopped canned tomatoes with their juice
2	large bay leaves
⅛	teaspoon cayenne pepper, or to taste
	Salt and ground black pepper
4 ½	cups Fish Stock (page 67) or Cheater's Fish Stock (page 69)
3	tablespoons golden raisins
3	pounds white-flesh fish fillets, rinsed, patted dry, and cut into 3- to 4-ounce pieces
12	large green olives, pitted and quartered lengthwise
¼	cup pine nuts, toasted
2	tablespoons minced fresh mint leaves

⁘ INSTRUCTIONS:

1. Heat oil in large soup kettle. Add onions and garlic and cook over medium heat until softened, about 5 minutes. Add wine and simmer until reduced by half, 2 to 3 minutes.

Add tomatoes, bay leaves, cayenne pepper, and salt and pepper to taste. Bring to boil, reduce heat, and simmer until mixture has thickened to tomato sauce consistency, 15 to 20 minutes.

2. Add fish stock and raisins and bring to boil. Reduce heat to simmer and adjust seasonings with salt, pepper, and cayenne to taste.

3. Add fish pieces to stew and simmer, stirring a few times to ensure even cooking, for 5 minutes. Remove kettle from heat, cover, and let stand until fish is just cooked through, about 5 minutes. Stir in olives, nuts, and mint. Discard bay leaves and serve immediately.

Zarzuela

➤ **NOTE:** *Shellfish replaces fish in this Spanish stew. Lobster bodies and shrimp shells can be used in the fish stock if desired. Serves six to eight.*

2	tablespoons olive oil
2	medium onions, diced
2	medium red bell peppers, stemmed, seeded, and diced
3	large garlic cloves, minced
2	ounces prosciutto, minced
½	cup coarse-ground toasted almonds
⅛	teaspoon saffron threads, crumbled (*see* figure 10, page 59)
½	cup dry white wine
2	cups chopped canned tomatoes with their juice
2	large bay leaves
⅛	teaspoon cayenne pepper, or to taste
	Salt and ground black pepper
4½	cups Fish Stock (page 67) or Cheater's Fish Stock (page 69)
1	lobster (about 1½ pounds), cut into pieces (*see* figures 14–19)
12	littleneck clams, scrubbed

(continued on next page)

(continued from previous page)

12	**mussels, scrubbed and debearded**
12	**large shrimp, shelled but tails on**
½	**pound sea scallops (halved if very large)**
¼	**cup minced fresh parsley leaves**

I N S T R U C T I O N S :

1. Heat oil in large soup kettle. Add onions, bell peppers, and garlic and cook over medium heat until softened, about 10 minutes. Add prosciutto, almonds, and saffron and sauté to coat with oil, about 1 minute. Add wine and simmer until reduced by half, 2 to 3 minutes. Add tomatoes, bay leaves, cayenne pepper, and salt and pepper to taste. Bring to boil, reduce heat, and simmer until mixture has thickened to tomato sauce consistency, 15 to 20 minutes.

2. Add fish stock and bring to boil. Reduce heat to simmer and adjust seasonings with salt, pepper, and cayenne to taste.

3. Add lobster pieces and clams and simmer for 3 minutes. Add mussels and simmer for 2 minutes. Add shrimp and scallops and simmer for 3 minutes, removing clams and mussels as they open and transferring them to soup plates. Stir in parsley, discard bay leaves, and serve immediately.

Figure 14.

*Freeze the lobster for 5 to 10 minutes to make it easier to handle.
Remove the lobster from the freezer and place the point
of a chef's knife at the center of the cross on the lobster's head.
Stab to kill.*

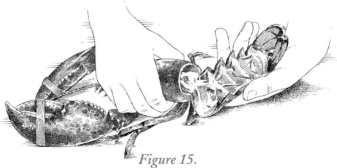

Figure 15.
Twist the tail from the body to separate them.

81

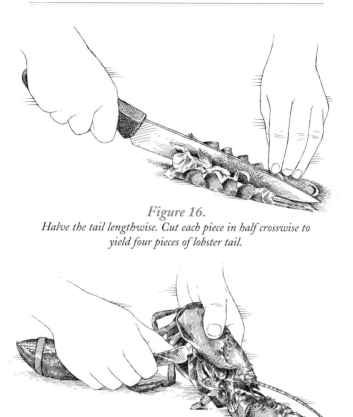

Figure 16.
Halve the tail lengthwise. Cut each piece in half crosswise to
yield four pieces of lobster tail.

Figure 17.
Twist the claws to separate them from the body.
(Save the body to make stock.)

82

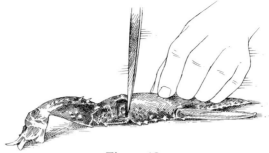

Figure 18.
Cut through each claw at the first joint to separate the meaty
portion of the claw from the long, tubular portion of the claw.

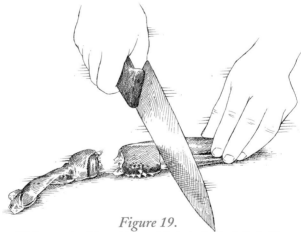

Figure 19.
With a couple of sharp blows with the back of a chef's knife,
crack each piece of the claw.

chapter five

VEGETABLE STEWS

ANY VEGETABLE STEWS CAN TASTE one-dimensional, much like a pan of sautéed vegetables with some broth. There is nothing wrong with these "stews," but they lack the intensity of a good meat, chicken, or fish stew. The biggest challenge when making vegetable stew is figuring out how to create a rich, deep flavor. This task is even harder if you want to make a vegetarian (that is, no chicken stock) vegetable stew. However, we have had some good vegetarian stews in the past—dishes worth eating even if you like meat—and wanted to figure out what makes some vegetarian stews delicious and others bland and insipid.

We started our testing by preparing a number of basic vegetable stews and devising a composite recipe. From early tests, we preferred stews that started with onions, carrots, and celery sautéed in oil. (We tested butter but preferred the lighter flavor of olive oil with the vegetables.) For maximum flavor, we found it best to mince these vegetables and let them brown. We also found the addition of garlic and a strong herb, such as rosemary or thyme, added further depth to this base for the stew.

At this point, the larger vegetables, those which would hold their shape during cooking and form the backbone of the stew, could be added. High-moisture vegetables that are usually sautéed, such as mushrooms, red onions, fennel, eggplant, bell peppers, and zucchini, should be added at this point. The pot can then be deglazed with a little wine. We found that red wine overpowered the vegetables and vastly preferred white wine. We also found that too much wine will make the stew boozy, no doubt because of the relatively short simmering time for vegetable stews. However, when we omitted white wine we felt the stew tasted flat. A half cup adds just the right amount of flavor and acidity to a vegetable stew.

Once the wine has reduced, it is time to add the other liquids along with root vegetables. We experimented with various liquids and liked the combination of vegetable stock and tomatoes. Homemade vegetable stock makes a delicious stew, but canned products are fine as long as you shop carefully. Vegetable stews tend to be sweet, so avoid stocks that are more sweet than savory. You can almost tell by looking at the stock how it will taste. If the color is bright orange, the stock was made with a lot of carrots and will be achingly sweet. We found the shockingly orange canned vegetable stocks made by Swanson and College Inn to be quite sweet. We had better luck when shopping at our local natural food store. We particularly liked an organic stock made by Pacific Foods of Oregon. It comes packaged in an aseptic carton and has a good, balanced vegetable flavor.

In addition to stock, we like to add tomatoes, both for flavor and color. The acidity helps balance some of the sweetness of the vegetables and the red color keeps vegetable stews from looking dull or brown.

We tested porcini soaking liquid and cream and found that both are too intense for an all-purpose vegetable stew. The one exception was a root vegetable stew that was quite sweet and needed some additional savory elements. The smoky, meaty flavor of the porcini helps balance the sweetness of carrots and butternut squash. We also liked some cream in this rich winter stew. However, we found that the cream muted the flavor of more delicate spring and summer vegetables such as zucchini, eggplant, and asparagus.

Some sources suggest thickening vegetable stews with flour (like meat stews) or by stirring in a cornstarch slurry when the stew is almost done. However, both methods assume that the vegetables have been cooked in an abundant amount of liquid that needs thickening. We found that vegetable stews taste watered down when the vegetables are cooked in too much liquid. We found it best to cook the vegetables in just as much liquid as is necessary. While other stews are cooked covered, we prefer to cook vegetable stews partially covered to allow some of this liquid to reduce and concentrate in flavor. Cooking the stew with the cover ajar also allows the liquid to thicken up to a nice consistency.

For this reason (and because different vegetables must go into the pot at different times), we prefer to cook vegetable stews on top of the stove. This eliminates the problem of toughening vegetables by cooking at a high temperature, a constant worry when making meat, chicken, or fish stews. Vegetable stews can be simmered (not boiled, you don't want the veggies to fall apart) rather quickly, just until the vegetables are tender.

When the stew is almost done, delicate green vegetables such as asparagus and peas should be added. We found it best to add a little acid (either lemon juice or balsamic vinegar) just before serving the stew to balance the sweetness of the vegetables. A fresh herb finishes things off nicely.

Master Recipe

Vegetable Stew

➤ **NOTE:** *Portobello mushrooms give this all-purpose vegetable stew a rich, deep flavor that complements the flavor of the other vegetables. Serves six to eight.*

2   tablespoons olive oil

1   medium onion, minced

1   medium carrot, minced

1   medium celery stalk, minced

1   medium red onion, cut into ½-inch pieces

4   medium portobello mushrooms
    (about 1¼ pounds), stems discarded,
    caps halved and then sliced ½-inch-thick

10 ounces white button mushrooms, halved

2   medium garlic cloves, minced

1   teaspoon minced fresh rosemary

½   cup white wine

2   cups vegetable stock

1   cup chopped canned tomatoes with juice

1   bay leaf

4   large carrots, peeled and sliced ¼-inch thick

88

4 medium boiling potatoes, peeled and cut into
½-inch cubes

1 cup frozen peas (about 6 ounces), thawed

¼ cup minced fresh parsley leaves

1 tablespoon lemon juice

INSTRUCTIONS:

1. Heat oil over medium-high heat in large ovenproof Dutch oven. Add minced onion, carrot, and celery and sauté until vegetables begin to brown, about 10 minutes.

2. Add red onion to Dutch oven and sauté until softened, about 5 minutes. Add portobello and button mushrooms and sauté until liquid they release has evaporated, about 10 minutes. Add garlic and rosemary; cook for 30 seconds. Add wine, scraping up any browned bits that may have stuck to pot. Add stock, tomatoes, bay leaf, carrots, and potatoes, and bring to a simmer. Simmer, partially covered, until carrots and potatoes are tender, about 30 minutes.

3. Turn off heat, stir in peas, cover, and allow to stand for 5 minutes. Stir in parsley and lemon juice, discard bay leaf, adjust seasonings, and serve.

Spring Vegetable Stew with Fennel and Asparagus

➤ **N O T E :** *An equal amount of shelled and skinned fava beans would make a nice substitution for the peas. Serves six to eight.*

2	tablespoons olive oil
1	medium onion, minced
1	medium carrot, minced
1	medium celery stalk, minced
1	medium red onion, cut into ½-inch pieces
1	small fennel bulb cut into ½-inch pieces, tough parts and stalks discarded
2	medium garlic cloves, minced
1	teaspoon minced fresh thyme leaves
½	cup white wine
2	cups vegetable stock
1	cup chopped canned tomatoes with their juice
1	bay leaf
2	large carrots, peeled and sliced ¼-inch thick
2	medium boiling potatoes, peeled and cut into ½-inch cubes
8	medium asparagus spears, tough ends discarded and cut on the bias into 1-inch pieces
1	cup frozen peas (about 6 ounces), thawed
¼	cup minced fresh basil leaves
1	tablespoon lemon juice

⠿ INSTRUCTIONS:

1. Heat oil over medium-high heat in large ovenproof Dutch oven. Add minced onion, carrot, and celery and sauté until vegetables begin to brown, about 10 minutes.

2. Add red onion and fennel to Dutch oven and sauté until they begin to brown, about 10 minutes. Add garlic and thyme and continue to cook for 30 seconds. Add wine, scraping up any browned bits that may have stuck to pot. Add stock, tomatoes, bay leaf, carrots, and potatoes, and bring to a simmer. Simmer, partially covered, for 25 minutes. Add asparagus and continue to simmer until vegetables are tender, about 3 minutes.

3. Turn off heat, stir in peas, cover, and allow to stand for 5 minutes. Stir in basil and lemon juice, discard bay leaf, adjust seasonings, and serve.

Vegetable Stew with Eggplant, Red Pepper, Zucchini, and Chickpeas

➤ NOTE: *This summer stew, which highlights the flavors of a traditional ratatouille, is delicious on its own or served over couscous. Serves six to eight.*

3½	tablespoons olive oil
1	medium onion, minced
1	medium carrot, minced
1	medium celery stalk, minced
1	large red bell pepper, stemmed, seeded, and cut into ½-inch dice
2	medium garlic cloves, minced
1	teaspoon minced fresh rosemary
2	medium zucchini (about ¾ pound), quartered lengthwise and cut into ½-inch chunks
1	large eggplant (about 1 pound), cut into ½-inch dice
½	cup white wine
2	cups vegetable stock
1	cup chopped canned tomatoes with their juice
1	bay leaf
1	15-ounce can cooked chickpeas, drained and rinsed (about 1¾ cups)
¼	cup minced fresh mint leaves
2	teaspoons balsamic vinegar

INSTRUCTIONS:

1. Heat 2 tablespoons oil over medium-high heat in large ovenproof Dutch oven. Add minced onion, carrot, and celery and sauté until vegetables begin to brown, about 10 minutes.

2. Add red pepper, garlic, and rosemary to Dutch oven and cook for 30 seconds. Scrape vegetables into bowl. Add ½ tablespoon oil and zucchini and sauté until softened, about 7 minutes. Scrape zucchini into bowl with other vegetables. Add remaining tablespoon oil and eggplant and sauté until softened, about 5 minutes. Add vegetables in bowl back to pot. Add wine, scraping up any browned bits that may have stuck to pot. Add stock, tomatoes, and bay leaf, and bring to a simmer. Simmer, partially covered, until vegetables are tender, about 15 minutes.

3. Turn off heat, stir in chickpeas, cover, and allow to stand for 5 minutes. Stir in mint and balsamic vinegar, discard bay leaf, adjust seasonings, and serve.

Root Vegetable Stew with Porcini and Cream

➤ N O T E : *Turnips, potatoes, carrots, and butternut squash make this stew hearty and satisfying. The porcini give the stew a smoky, meaty flavor that balances the sweetness of the vegetables. Serves six to eight.*

½	ounce dried porcini mushrooms
2	tablespoons olive oil
1	medium onion, minced
1	medium carrot, minced
1	medium celery stalk, minced
2	medium garlic cloves, minced
1	teaspoon minced fresh rosemary
½	cup white wine
1½	cups vegetable stock
1	cup chopped canned tomatoes with their juice
½	cup heavy cream
1	bay leaf
2	medium turnips, peeled and cut into ¾-inch cubes
2	large carrots, peeled and sliced ¼-inch thick
2	medium boiling potatoes, peeled and cut into ½ -inch cubes
½	small butternut squash (about 1 pound), peeled, seeded, and cut into ½ -inch cubes
¼	cup minced fresh parsley leaves or snipped chives

1   tablespoon lemon juice

⁞⁞ INSTRUCTIONS:

1. Place porcini in small bowl and cover with ¾ cup hot tap water. Soak until softened, about 20 minutes. Carefully lift mushrooms from liquid with fork and pick through to remove any foreign debris. Wash mushrooms under cold water if they feel gritty, then chop. Strain soaking liquid through sieve lined with paper towel or coffee filter. Reserve mushrooms and strained soaking liquid separately.

2. Heat oil over medium-high heat in large ovenproof Dutch oven. Add minced onion, carrot, and celery and sauté until vegetables begin to brown, about 10 minutes.

3. Add chopped porcini, garlic, and rosemary to Dutch oven and continue to cook for 30 seconds. Add wine, scraping up any browned bits that may have stuck to pot. Add strained porcini liquid, stock, tomatoes, cream, bay leaf, turnips, carrots, and potatoes, and bring to a simmer. Simmer, partially covered, for 25 minutes. Add squash and continue simmering until vegetables are tender, 10 to 15 minutes.

4. Stir in parsley and lemon juice, discard bay leaf, adjust seasonings, and serve.

index